Punch Cartoons of the Great War

Various

Alpha Editions

This edition published in 2024

ISBN 9789362926791

Design and Setting By

Alpha Editions

www.alphaedis.com

Email - info@alphaedis.com

As per information held with us this book is in Public Domain.
This book is a reproduction of an important historical work.
Alpha Editions uses the best technology to reproduce historical work
in the same manner it was first published to preserve its original nature.
Any marks or number seen are left intentionally to preserve.

Contents

THE DAYS PRECEDING THE WAR	- 1 -
THE STRUGGLE	- 18 -
UNCLE SAM	- 45 -
THE COMEDIES OF THE GREAT TRAGEDY	- 50 -
WOMEN AND CHILDREN FIRST	- 71 -
THE NEW RAKE'S PROGRESS—UNSER KAISER	- 79 -
THE RAIDER	- 90 -
THE UNSPEAKABLE TURK	- 93 -
ITALIA!	- 106 -

THE DAYS PRECEDING THE WAR

A WISE WARNING

DÆDALUS BISMARCK (*Political Parent of* WILHELM ICARUS).

"My son, observe the middle path to fly, And fear to sink too low, or rise too high. Here the sun melts, there vapours damp your force, Between the two extremes direct your course.

"Nor on the bear, nor on boötes gaze, Nor on sword-arm'd orion's dangerous rays: But follow me, thy guide, with watchful sight, And, as I steer, direct thy cautious Flight."

OVID, *"Metamorphoses," Book VIII., Fable III.*

October 6, 1888.

THE HAUNTED SHIP

(Twenty-five years after "Dropping the Pilot.")

GHOST OF THE OLD PILOT. "I WONDER IF HE WOULD DROP ME *NOW*!"

(April 1st is the hundredth anniversary of BISMARCK'S birth.)

March 31, 1915.

L'ENFANT TERRIBLE

CHORUS IN THE STERN. "DON'T GO ON LIKE THAT—OR YOU'LL UPSET US ALL!!"

May 10, 1890.

THE IMPERIAL JACK-IN-THE-BOX

CHORUS (*Everybody*). " EVERYTHING IN ORDER EVERYWHERE! O! WHAT A SURPRISE! SOLD AGAIN!"

January 20, 1893.

THE MODERN ALEXANDER'S FEAST; OR, THE POWER OF SOUND

"With ravished ears,The Monarch hears,Assumes the God,Affects to nod,And seems to shake the spheres!"

March 5, 1892.

THE STORY OF FIDGETY WILHELM
(Up-to-date version of "Struwwelpeter.")

"Let me see if Wilhelm canBe a little gentleman;Let me see if he is ableTo sit still for once at table!"

"But fidgety WillHe won't sit still."

Just like any bucking horse."Wilhelm! We are getting cross!"

February 1, 1896.

A NEW RÔLE

IMPERIAL "MANAGER-ACTOR" (*who has cast himself for a leading part in "Un Voyage en Chine," sotto voce*).

"UM—HA! WITH JUST A FEW ADDITIONAL TOUCHES HERE AND THERE, I SHALL MAKE A FIRST-RATE EMPEROR OF CHINA!"

January 15, 1898.

ON TOUR

(Tangier, March 31.)

KAISER WILHELM *(as the Moor of Potsdam) sings:—*

"'Unter den Linden'—always at Home,'Under the Lime-light' wherever I roam!"

April 5, 1905.

COOK'S CRUSADER

IMPERIAL KNIGHT TEMPLAR (*the German Emperor—to* SALADIN). "What!! The Christian Powers putting pressure upon You, my dear Friend!! Horrible! I can't think how People can do such things!"

October 15, 1898.

NOT IN THE PICTURE

SCENE—*On shore, during the visit of the British Fleet to Brest.*

MR. PUNCH (*Photographer, suavely, to the* KAISER). "Just a leetle further back, please, Sir. Your shadow still rather interferes with the group."

July 12, 1905.

THE SOWER OF TARES

(AFTER MILLAIS)

August 23, 1905.

"ISOLATION"

PEACE (*attending the Inter-Parliamentary Congress at Berlin*). "Everybody else seems to be my friend; why do you stand aloof?"

GERMAN KAISER. "But haven't I always said that I was your friend?"

PEACE. "Yes; but can't you do something to prove it?"

September 23, 1908.

THE TEUTONISING OF TURKEY

GERMAN KAISER. "Good Bird!"

October 5, 1910.

HARMONY

[THE GERMAN EMPEROR *has been patronising the Centenary of* KRUPP'S *Gun Factory*]

August 14, 1912.

THE BLIND SIDE

GERMAN OFFICER: "Glad to hear you're going to fortify your sea-front. Very dangerous people, these English."

DUTCHMAN: "But it will cost much."

GERMAN OFFICER: "Ah, but see what you save on the Eastern Frontier, where there's nobody but us."

January 11, 1911.

THE STRUGGLE

WELL MET!

GREAT BRITAIN JOINS HER ALLIES IN THE FIELD

August 19, 1914.

BRAVO, BELGIUM!

August 12, 1914.

FOR FRIENDSHIP AND HONOUR

August 12, 1914.

AT THE POST OF HONOUR

LIBERTY (*to Belgium*). "TAKE COMFORT. YOUR COURAGE IS VINDICATED; YOUR WRONGS SHALL BE AVENGED."

September 2, 1914.

INDIA FOR THE KING!

September 9, 1914.

HAIL! RUSSIA!

September 16, 1914.

BOER AND BRITON TOO

GENERAL BOTHA (*composing telegram to the* KAISER). "Just off to repel another raid. Your customary wire of congratulation should be addressed: 'British Headquarters—German South-west Africa.'"

September 30, 1914.

A NORTH SEA CHANTEY

(*To the tune of "Tipperary."*)

JACK. "IT'S A LONG, LONG WAIT FOR WILLIAM'S NAVY, BUT MY HEART'S RIGHT HERE"

October 14, 1914.

THE ROAD TO RUSSIA

October 7, 1914.

UNCONQUERABLE

THE KAISER. "SO, YOU SEE—YOU'VE LOST EVERYTHING."
THE KING OF THE BELGIANS. "NOT MY SOUL."

October 21, 1914.

A PLAIN DUTY

BRITANNIA (*to Holland*). "MY RESOURCES AND MY OBLIGATIONS ARE GREATER THAN YOURS; LET THIS SERVICE FALL UPON ME."

[The number of Belgian refugees in Holland is probably ten times as great as the number in England.]

October 28, 1914.

FOREWARNED

Zeppelin (*as "The Fat Boy"*). "'I WANTS TO MAKE YOUR FLESH CREEP.'"

John Bull. "RIGHT-O!"

November 4, 1914.

THE EXCURSIONIST

Scene: Ticket Office at ⸺ (*censored*).

Tripper Wilhelm. "FIRST CLASS TO PARIS."
Clerk. "LINE BLOCKED."

Wilhelm. "THEN MAKE IT WARSAW."
Clerk. "LINE BLOCKED."

WILHELM. "WELL, WHAT ABOUT CALAIS?"
CLERK. "LINE BLOCKED."

WILHELM. "HANG IT! I *MUST GO SOMEWHERE*! I PROMISED MY PEOPLE I WOULD."

November 4, 1914.

THE EAGLE COMIQUE

KAISER (*reviving old Music-hall refrain*). "HAS ANYBODY HERE SEEN *CALAIS*?"

November 18, 1914.

GOOD HUNTING

A CHIP OFF THE OLD BLOCK

November 18, 1914.

MEN OF FEW WORDS

GRAND DUKE NICHOLAS. "ÇA MARCHE?"

GENERAL JOFFRE. "ASSEZ BIEN. ET CHEZ VOUS?"

GRAND DUKE. "PAS MAL."

December 2, 1914.

THE KING AT THE FRONT

"TOMMY" (*having learned the language*). "VIVE LE ROI!"

December 9, 1914.

THE INNOCENT

CROWN PRINCE. "THIS OUGHT TO MAKE FATHER LAUGH!"

[In an alleged interview the CROWN PRINCE is reported to have said, "As to being a war agitator, I am truly sorry that people don't know me better. There is no 'War Party' in Germany now—nor has there ever been."]

December 9, 1914.

KILLED!

[WITH *Mr. Punch's* COMPLIMENTS TO GENERAL BOTHA]

December 16, 1914.

FULFILMENT

AUSTRIA. "I SAID ALL ALONG THIS WAS GOING TO BE A PUNITIVE EXPEDITION"

December 23, 1914.

THE BREAKING OF THE SPELL
STEINBACH, JANUARY 3, 1915

January 13, 1915.

AN AWFUL WARNING

Austria (to Rumania). "NOW, BE CAREFUL! REMEMBER WHAT I DID TO SERBIA!"

January 20, 1915.

THE OUTCAST

A PLACE IN THE SHADOW

February 19, 1915.

A PAINFUL REFLECTION

AUSTRIA. "HEAVENS! AM I REALLY AS BAD AS THAT? TAKE IT AWAY."

[It seems to be dawning upon Vienna that the armies of Austria have not been consistently victorious.]

April 14, 1915.

CANADA!
YPRES: APRIL 22-24, 1915

May 5, 1915.

THE NEW ARMY TO THE FRONT

December 30, 1914.

UNCLE SAM

NOTHING DOING

IMPERIAL DACHSHUND. "HERE I'VE BEEN SITTING UP AND DOING TRICKS FOR THE BEST PART OF SEVEN WEEKS, AND YOU TAKE NO MORE NOTICE OF ME THAN IF———"

UNCLE SAM. "CUT IT OUT!"

September 23, 1914.

AS BETWEEN FRIENDS

BRITISH LION. "PLEASE DON'T LOOK AT ME LIKE THAT, SAM. *YOU*'RE NOT THE EAGLE I'M UP AGAINST."

January 6, 1915.

A BRAZEN BAND

IMPERIAL CONDUCTOR. "STICK TO IT, TIRPITZ; KEEP ON MELTING THEIR HEARTS!"

March 31, 1915.

REJECTED ADDRESSES

KAISER (*to America*). "Perhaps it was right to dissemble your love; But why did you kick me downstairs?"

April 21, 1915.

THE RESOURCEFUL LOVER

TEUTON TROUBADOUR (*serenading the fair Columbia*). "IF SHE WON'T LISTEN TO MY LOVE-SONGS, I'LL TRY HER WITH A BRICK!"

February 17, 1915.

THE COMEDIES OF THE GREAT TRAGEDY

STUDY OF A PRUSSIAN HOUSEHOLD HAVING ITS MORNING HATE

February 24, 1915.

GERMAN BIRD. "I SEE IT DOESN'T SAY ANYTHING ABOUT EAGLES."

August 26, 1914.

THE HOHENZOLLERN (*megaphonically*). "TAKE COURAGE, MY BRAVE GERMANS. YOUR KAISER IS PREPARED TO SACRIFICE A MILLION OF YOU."

August 26, 1914.

GERMAN KAISER. "LET US PREY."

September 9, 1914.

THE HUNTER HUNTED

[With acknowledgments to Mr. J. C. DOLLMAN.]

September 16, 1914.

Admiral of the Atlantic (to himself). "IT IS MY IMPERIAL PLEASURE TO PRESENT YOU WITH THE ORDER OF THE MASTHEAD BROOM (FIRST CLASS) IN RECOGNITION OF YOUR CONSPICUOUS SUCCESS IN SWEEPING THE SEAS."

September 23, 1914.

The Wolff. "Good morning, my dear Little Red Riding Hood. Wouldn't you like me to tell you one of my pretty tales?"

Little Miss Holland. "Thanks; but I'm *not* Little Red Riding Hood, and I don't want any of your fairy stories."

September 23, 1914.

A GARGOYLE OF NOTRE DAME DE PARIS

(With acknowledgements to the etching by M. Méryon.)

Spirits of evil, when they're thrownOut of a Church, are turned to stone;

But the above was petrifiedEven before he got inside.

October 28, 1914.

LATEST DEVICE OF THE ENEMY

Learning to sing "It's a long, long way to Tipperary" for the purpose of deceiving the Allies.

November 4, 1914.

A Prussian Court-painter earning an Iron Cross by painting pictures in praise of the Fatherland for neutral consumption

November 11, 1914.

UNRECORDED EVENTS IN THE HISTORY OF THE WAR

GERMAN SOLDIERS BEING ROUSED TO ENTHUSIASM BY THE "HYMN OF HATE"

December 16, 1914.

THE IRON CROSS EPIDEMIC

Captain of a German cruiser, hurrying home after shelling health-resort, gives orders to lighten the ship for the sake of speed.

December 23, 1914.

HOW TO BRING UP A HUN

THE TEUTONIC SUBSTITUTE FOR MILK

November 11, 1914.

Turkey. "Looks very tempting and fruity; but what I want to know is, who's going to pay the doctor's bill if complications ensue?"

September 9, 1914.

FAITH

December 9, 1914.

Voice on telephone (from Berlin). "WELL, HAVE YOU DAMMED THE SUEZ CANAL YET?"

Turk. "YES—OFTEN!"

February 10, 1915.

Turk. "I SAY, YOU FELLOWS! DO YOU SEE THE OTHER ALLIES ARE POOLING THEIR FUNDS? CAPITAL IDEA!"

February 17, 1915.

"IN THE SPRING A YOUNG MAN'S FANCY——"

THE CROWN PRINCE. "I DON'T BELIEVE I WAS MEANT TO WIN BATTLES; I BELIEVE I WAS MEANT TO BE LOVED."

April 28, 1915.

GERMAN KAISER. "WE ARE NOT SATISFIED WITH OUR MOUSTACHE; IT SEEMS TO NEED SUPPORT ON THE EASTERN SIDE."

September 2, 1914.

FOR NEUTRAL CONSUMPTION

September 2, 1914.

WILLIAM THE GALLANT

THE KAISER, BY GIFTS OF ROSES, HAS BEEN TRYING TO INGRATIATE HIMSELF WITH THE GRAND DUCHESS OF LUXEMBOURG, WHOSE COUNTRY HE HAS INVADED IN DEFIANCE OF TREATY OBLIGATIONS.

January 20, 1915.

WOMEN AND CHILDREN FIRST

THE TRIUMPH OF "CULTURE"

August 26, 1914.

GOD (AND THE WOMEN) OUR SHIELD!
STUDY OF A GERMAN GENTLEMAN GOING INTO ACTION

September 9, 1914.

DISHONOURED

CAPTAIN OF THE *EMDEN*. "DIRTY WORK!"

December 30, 1914.

THE FLIGHT THAT FAILED

THE EMPEROR. "WHAT! NO BABES, SIRRAH?"

THE MURDERER. "ALAS! SIRE, NONE."

THE EMPEROR. "WELL, THEN, NO BABES, NO IRON CROSSES."

[Exit murderer, discouraged.]

January 27, 1915.

THE BREAD-WINNER

March 3, 1915.

A GREAT NAVAL TRIUMPH

GERMAN SUBMARINE OFFICER. "THIS OUGHT TO MAKE THEM JEALOUS IN THE SISTER SERVICE. BELGIUM SAW NOTHING BETTER THAN THIS."

April 7, 1915.

THE ELIXIR OF HATE

KAISER. "'FAIR IS FOUL, AND FOUL IS FAIR; HOVER THROUGH THE FOG AND FILTHY AIR.'"

May 5, 1915.

THE NEW RAKE'S PROGRESS—UNSER KAISER

THE COMING OF THE COSSACKS

WILHELM II. "WHAT IS THIS DISTANT RUMBLING THAT I HEAR? DOUBTLESS THE PLAUDITS OF MY PEOPLE!"

August 26, 1914.

THE WORLD'S ENEMY

THE KAISER. "WHO GOES THERE?"

SPIRIT OF CARNAGE. "A FRIEND—YOUR ONLY ONE."

August 19, 1914.

MADE IN GERMANY

KAISER. "I'M NOT QUITE SATISFIED WITH THE SWORD. PERHAPS, AFTER ALL, THE PEN IS MIGHTIER!"

September 16, 1914.

THE GREAT ILLUSION

KAISER. "MY POOR BIRD, WHAT *HAS* HAPPENED TO YOUR TAIL-FEATHERS?"

GERMAN EAGLE. "CAN YOU BEAR THE TRUTH, SIRE?"

KAISER. "IF IT'S NOT FOR PUBLICATION."

GERMAN EAGLE. "IT'S LIKE THIS, THEN. YOU TOLD ME THE BRITISH LION WAS CONTEMPTIBLE. WELL—HE WASN'T!"

September 23, 1914.

THE GREAT GOTH

DESIGN FOR A STAINED-GLASS WINDOW IN A NEO-GOTHIC CATHEDRAL AT POTSDAM

September 30, 1914.

GIVING THE SHOW AWAY

GERMAN PRESS BUREAU PHOTOGRAPHER. "COSTUME PERFECT, SIRE—ACCESSORIES ADMIRABLE; BUT, IN VIEW OF ALL THESE 'VICTORIES,' DARE WE SUGGEST THAT THE *EXPRESSION* MIGHT BE JUST A TOUCH MORE *JUBILANT?*"

October 14, 1914.

THE LIMIT

Scene: THE COAST OF BELGIUM

THE KAISER. "'WHAT ARE THE WILD WAVES SAYING?'"

WILD WAVES. "WE WERE JUST SAYING, 'THUS FAR, AND NO FARTHER!'"

October 28, 1914.

A CHRONIC COMPLAINT

AIDE-DE-CAMP. "'THE ENGLISH FORCE, SO PLEASE YOU.'"

KAISER. "'TAKE THY FACE HENCE ... I AM SICK AT HEART.'"

MACBETH, ACT V., SC. 3.

December 2, 1914.

THE WHITEWASHERS

KAISER. "LAY IT ON, MY WORTHY PROFESSORS—LAY IT ON THICK! I WANT EVERY DROP OF IT."

January 20, 1915.

WILFUL MURDER

THE KAISER. "TO THE DAY——"
DEATH. "——OF RECKONING!"

May 19, 1915.

THE RAIDER

THE RETURN OF THE RAIDER

KAISER. "WELL, I *AM* SURPRISED!"

TIRPITZ. "SO WERE WE."

February 3, 1915.

SOUND AND FURY

KAISER. "IS ALL MY HIGH SEAS FLEET SAFELY LOCKED UP?"

ADMIRAL VON TIRPITZ. "PRACTICALLY ALL, SIRE."

KAISER. "THEN LET THE STARVATION OF ENGLAND BEGIN!"

February 17, 1915.

RUNNING AMOK

GERMAN BULL. "I KNOW I'M MAKING A ROTTEN EXHIBITION OF MYSELF; BUT I SHALL TELL EVERYBODY I WAS GOADED INTO IT."

February 24, 1915.

THE UNSPEAKABLE TURK

OUT OF BOUNDS

JOHN BULL. "SHOO! SHOO!"

May 9, 1906.

ARMAGEDDON: A DIVERSION

TURKEY. "GOOD! IF ONLY ALL THOSE OTHER CHRISTIAN NATIONS GET AT ONE ANOTHER'S THROATS, I MAY HAVE A DOG'S CHANCE YET."

December 4, 1912.

SETTLED

DAME EUROPA. "You've always been the most troublesome boy in the school. Now go and consolidate yourself."

TURKEY. "Please, ma'am, what does that mean?"

DAME EUROPA. "It means going into that corner—and stopping there!"

April 2, 1913.

HIS MASTER'S VOICE

THE KAISER (*to Turkey, reassuringly*). "LEAVE EVERYTHING TO ME. ALL YOU'VE GOT TO DO IS TO EXPLODE."

TURKEY. "YES, I QUITE SEE THAT. BUT WHERE SHALL *I* BE WHEN IT'S ALL OVER?"

November 11, 1914.

THE EUPHEMISTS

KAISER. "I say, how are you going to explain away the surrender of your army corps in the Caucasus?"

SULTAN OF TURKEY. "Nothing simpler. I shall say, 'Our gallant troops determined to embarrass the enemy's commissariat, and carried out their object with overwhelming success."

KAISER. "Splendid! Couldn't have put it better myself."

SULTAN. "My dear boy, we were in the business ages and ages before you were thought of."

January 13, 1915.

THE GOD IN THE CART

(*An Unrehearsed Effect.*)

TURKEY. "I'm getting a bit fed up with this. I shall kick soon."

AUSTRIA. "Well, I was thinking of lying down."

January 6, 1915.

THE RIDDLE OF THE SANDS

TURKISH CAMEL. "WHERE TO?"

GERMAN OFFICER. "EGYPT."

CAMEL. "GUESS AGAIN."

February 10, 1915.

German Sentry. "WHO GOES THERE?"
Turk. "A FRIEND—CURSE YOU!"

January 20, 1915.

THE DISSEMBLERS

[JANUARY 27TH]

EMPEROR OF AUSTRIA. "NOW WHAT DO WE REALLY WANT TO SAY?"

SULTAN OF TURKEY. "WELL, OF COURSE, WE COULDN'T SAY *THAT*; NOT ON HIS BIRTHDAY."

January 27, 1915.

WILLIAM O' THE WISP

March 3, 1915.

THE REVERSION

Turkey. "I'M GIVING UP THIS BED, WILLIAM. WON'T YOU TAKE MY PLACE?"

April 7, 1915.

"'HE'S AS WILLING AS A CHRISTIAN; STRIKE ME BLIND IF HE ISN'T,' SAID SIKES."

Oliver Twist, Chap. xvi.

(*With apologies to the late Fred Barnard.*)

November 4, 1914.

ITALIA!

ON THE FENCE

ALL-HIGHEST (*to certain Neutrals*). "ABOUT—TURN!" [They sit tight.]

March 17, 1915.

VICARIOUS GENEROSITY

KAISER. "SHOULD YOU WANT SOME MORE FEATHERS, I KNOW A TWO-HEADED EAGLE"

March 24, 1915.

THE AWAKENING

PRINCE VON BÜLOW (*to Italy*). "STOP, STOP, SIGNORA! YOU'RE SUPPOSED TO BE *MESMERISED*—NOT *MOBILISED*!"

April 28, 1915.

ON WITH THE NEW HATE

May 12, 1915.

www.ingramcontent.com/pod-product-compliance
Ingram Content Group UK Ltd.
Pitfield, Milton Keynes, MK11 3LW, UK
UKHW041124150225
455111UK00004B/373